An Introduction to the
Business-Within-a-Business
Paradigm

*a vision of how
organizations should work*

by

N. Dean Meyer

An Introduction to the Business-Within-a-Business Paradigm: a vision of how organizations should work

Meyer, N. Dean

Key words: organization design, vision, governance, entrepreneurship, empowerment, shared services.

NDMA Publishing
641 Danbury Road, Suite D
Ridgefield, CT 06877 USA

203-431-0029
ndma@ndma.com

ISBN   1-892606-19-4

Printed in the United States of America.

CONTENTS

FIGURES

An Introduction to the Business-Within-a-Business Paradigm

*a vision of how
organizations should work*

1. Introduction

Building a high-performance organization should be every executive's top priority — as important as formulating brilliant strategies, hiring and inspiring the right people, and making tough decisions.

Effective leaders build organizations that tap every bright mind, such that everybody thinks creatively about business strategies, makes sound business decisions, and coordinates their work with their peers.

The visions these enlightened leaders put forward are not limited to business strategies. They also envision and create work environments and governance processes that maximize everyone's performance. In other words, great leaders build high-performance organizations.

What is a high-performance organization? By far the most powerful model for a high-performance organization is that of a *business within a business.*

The business-within-a-business (BWB) paradigm is *not* outsourcing or divestiture; it doesn't mean chargebacks, nor operating internal service functions as profit centers; and it doesn't imply an arm's-length relationship where support staff don't care about the well-being of the corporation.

The BWB paradigm simply means running internal service functions in an entrepreneurial fashion, and respecting clients' rights as internal customers.

The BWB paradigm brings out the best in people: customer focus, empowerment, teamwork, quality, judicious risk-taking, innovation, efficiency — all traits of successful entrepreneurs.

When people learn to think like entrepreneurs in an internal marketplace, they make better decisions. On any issue, when in doubt, ask yourself what an arm's-length business would do, and you'll find the BWB paradigm leads you to the right answer.

This monograph defines and explores the implications of the BWB paradigm, and suggests practical, systemic methods to implement it.

2. Concept

Each organization within a corporation exists to produce products and services. It "sells" its products and services to customers in its "market." *1* (The word "sell" in this context means "serve," whether or not money actually changes hands.)

An organization's market may be external customers, or it may be the rest of the company.

"A market is a collection of individual decision-making units, some of which desire to buy (demand) and some of which desire to sell (supply) a particular good or service."

Robert Haveman and Kenyon Knopf

A business within a business may "buy" help from peers within their immediate organization, or from other departments within the corporation — its suppliers.

Scope of Applicability

The BWB paradigm applies to every industry, as well as government and not-for-profit organizations. Even religious and volunteer organizations face the same challenges and work under the same laws of nature and human dynamics as do corporations.

1. I'll use the word "corporation" to include not-for-profit institutions and government entities. The word "organization" refers to any piece of a corporation — a department, a company, or an entire corporation, depending on the reader's purview.

In every industry, organizations must coordinate the efforts of a collection of people to deliver their products and services. They must take advantage of differing competencies, clarify account-abilities and authorities, optimally allocate scarce and precious resources (money and time), and coordinate everybody's efforts.

Furthermore, the BWB paradigm applies to every function. It's easy to see in the case of internal support functions such as information technologies, human resources, finance, law, and administration. But the concept is more broadly applicable.

Only a few departments within a corporation sell their products directly to external customers. They, in turn, depend on the goods and services produced by other departments within the corporation — internal service providers, both staff and line.

For example, consider the following tree-structured set of internal customer-supplier relationships:

Product managers are responsible for the profitability of divisions' product lines.

> *Product managers hire engineering to design their products.*

>> *Engineers buy computer-aided design tools from IT.*

> *Product managers buy manufacturing services to produce their products.*

>> *Manufacturing, in turn, needs manufacturing-engineering to prepare its plant to make the product.*

> *Product managers buy marketing programs to promote their products.*

> *Product managers commission the sales force to sell them.*

>> *The sales force buys various sales-support programs from marketing.*

A corporation is just like the country as a whole: a set of businesses buying from and selling to one another. All the various internal services combine to form the corporation's "value chain."

Components of a Business

As a business within a business, each internal service provider needs most of the elements found in any business as a whole.

* It must produce its products and services, and may provide customer service and training — its "operations" functions.

* It needs a diversity of types of specialists, such as engineers, to design, develop, and support its products and services.

* It needs coordinators to ensure an integrated product line.

* And, often neglected, it absolutely needs internal account representatives (client liaisons, i.e., sales and marketing) to facilitate effective partnerships with its internal customers and to help customers find high-payoff opportunities for its products and services (i.e., to align itself with customers' business strategies).

Granularity

The BWB paradigm is not limited to executives who run entire corporations or departments. It applies at every level, down to each small group of people who share a mission and product line.

Everyone at every level can think like an entrepreneur, and feel a sense of ownership of a small business, whether the group's customers are within their immediate department or throughout the company.

3. Competition

As a business, most every organization has intense competition. When speaking about a corporation in a competitive free market, this is obvious. But the same is true of support functions within corporations.

One form of competition is *outsourcing*.

If customers are dissatisfied with an internal service provider — either unhappy with the quality or value of its products and services, or displeased with the way the organization treats them — they may choose to buy from vendors and contractors rather than through internal staff.

Another form of competition is *decentralization*.

If customers don't want to do business with the corporation's central provider, they may choose to make its products and services themselves. They may simply do the work as part of their jobs, or they may go so far as to hire staff or contractors and start their own competing groups.

Of course, there are cases where clients will simply do without, missing potentially lucrative opportunities rather than do business with an organization they have difficulty working with.

In any case, the internal service provider loses market share.

Even if it seems as though the rest of the company *must* work through the organization (perhaps because of a mandate), the surest way to lose a monopoly is to behave as a monopolist.

In fact, a monopoly does not guarantee that the organization will remain in business. It only makes its market share either 100 percent or zero.

Without a monopoly, as internal customers become disgruntled, market share begins to dwindle. This is important news; it gives the organization an early-warning signal that it must change.

With a monopoly, however, pressure builds until dissatisfaction is so great that the entire organization is either outsourced or broken up and decentralized.

The bottom line is, every organization must earn the right to do business with its customers, be they external or internal, even if corporate policies dictate that clients must work through them.

4. Flow of Money

Many organizations receive a budget from their chain of command, and don't charge customers for their products and services.

This can mislead staff into thinking they exist to serve their boss rather than their customers.

Staff may think they are paid by the corporation to look after the interests of the corporation as a whole. They do what *they* think is best for the shareholders, rather than serve their internal customers and do what their customers think is best. This is the opposite of customer focus.

And since they've already gotten the money, they may not respect their customers right to decide what they'll buy, or recognize that they have competition. This leads to complacence and arrogance. Staff may even attempt to control customers by fighting any attempts to buy from external vendors.

This bureaucratic perspective, the antithesis of the BWB paradigm, undermines partnership, which threatens staff's ability to deliver strategic value.

In the BWB paradigm, budget is viewed as a *pre-paid account*. It's money put on deposit with the organization at the beginning of each year, to be used by customers throughout the year to buy its products and services.

In other words, an organization's budget is money in escrow, and doesn't belong to staff until they earn it by delivering their products and services.

The annual budget process fills these escrow accounts. Then a "purser" must be appointed — a person or committee who has the power to write checks out of this account, that is, to set priorities.

The purser should be a fair representative of the customers. It's inappropriate to appoint the provider organization as purser for its own resources. That would be like allowing IBM to decide what computers you'll buy.

In a BWB organization, each group begins the year with no budget. It spends money on staff compensation and other items. These expenses are offset by revenues, which are collected out of the escrow account when the organization delivers its products and services to its customers.

If customers want something, they must pay for it.

One way to pay is to convince the purser to set priorities such that the work is funded by the escrow account.

Another way is to give the organization money from the customer's own budget, which it can use to expand its capacity (through contractors and vendors) and provide work beyond what's covered by the budget. 2

In either case, everything has a cost to shareholders which must be paid by the customer.

Note that if a group can't do everything its customers demand, it's not the staff's fault. The corporation's spending power is limited. It's up to the group's customers to provide funding. Once the funding is there, the group's capacity is unlimited.

By the way, note that executives who wish to control costs have been frustrated with the ineffectiveness of headcount and expense caps. These artificial limits on the internal supply don't really reduce spending. They only drive costs up by forcing greater use of contractors, or forcing customers to use alternative sources such as decentralization and outsourcing.

2.   In advanced organizations, all work is funded through chargebacks. However, chargebacks are not recommended outside the context of an internal market economy, and it takes careful planning to implement a free market within a corporation. Even without chargebacks, a market effect can be created by appointing an organization's internal clients as its purser.

The only meaningful way to control costs is by constraining customers' spending power (demand), not by constraining staff's supply.

In a BWB organization, executives control spending by limiting customers' checkbooks, and then leave entrepreneurial staff free to expand their supply to meet all funded demand.

5. Differences from an Arm's-Length Business

The BWB paradigm has its limits. While an organization within a corporation can behave very much like an external vendor, it reports to the same shareholders as do its customers. Hence, some adjustments are appropriate.

1. Profits generally accrue to the customers, not the provider.

Let's assume that an organization produces its products and services at a cost that's below their market value. (If it doesn't, it deserves to be outsourced.)

As an external vendor, it would charge market prices and earn a profit. Internally, however, chargebacks are not all that common; and even when organizations do charge internal customers, the price is almost always set to cost rather than market.

It's not that internal service providers don't make a profit. When a product that has a market value of $10 is produced for $8, the shareholders have earned $2. The only difference is that the profits are recorded on the books of the customers, not the provider.

This means that it's difficult to measure return on equity, as the shareholders of external companies do. Instead, internal businesses are measured on market share, customer satisfaction, and competitive cost benchmarks (e.g., vendors prices and outsourcing bids).

2. A BWB is asked to do things for shareholders that would be inappropriate for external vendors to do.

Internal staff are often asked to do things for the benefit of the corporation as a whole, like setting standards and policies, managing vendors, and a service akin to "consumer reports" that includes vendor-product R&D and recommending safe, standard configurations to the company.

We term these corporate-good activities "subsidies."

They should be funded directly by the corporation, not imbedded in the organization's prices to customers. These are costs that would be incurred whether or not customers buy the organization's products and services; and imbedding these costs in its prices would put an internal entrepreneurship at a competitive disadvantage.

3. A BWB needs investment funding to buy infrastructure and make significant investments in its business.

When it makes significant capital investments in infrastructure, new lines of business, or major business improvements, an external company turns to its bank, shareholders, or venture capitalists for additional capitalization.

Internally, a BWB must get "venture" funding from the corporation through its budget.

Most corporations ask that the organization pay back venture funding through depreciation. Few demand interest on capital employed, although it would be appropriate to do so.

Whatever the payback method, ventures are amortized over time, not imbedded in this year's costs to customers.

4. When it comes to peers, internal entrepreneurs work through one another, not around one another.

If a supplier isn't performing, a corporation simply buys elsewhere. As long as other suppliers are available, a corporation doesn't really care if other companies fail.

Internally, the situation is a bit different. If a peer isn't offering the best deal, an internal entrepreneur doesn't let that other group sink while he or she looks outside for help. Instead, internal entrepreneurs help one another succeed, or escalate problems until the organization fixes them.

This short-term constraint on entrepreneurship is a long-term investment in the health of the entire organization.

6. Implications for Business Processes

For an organization to work, cross-boundary teamwork is essential. Corporations of "stove-pipe" independent companies, or departments of completely independent groups, may as well be broken up; they rarely generate enough synergies to justify the costs of the common oversight function.

In other words, business processes that cross organizational boundaries are how healthy organizations get their work done.

This takes more than team building and cordial relations. Effective cross-boundary processes (i.e., high-performance teamwork) require the following:

*   For every project or service, a team draws together just the right people from throughout the entire organization, without regard for structural boundaries.

*   Teams form laterally, without the need for top-management intervention, i.e., self-forming teams.

*   People on the team have clear individual accountabilities; they may help teammates succeed, but they don't meddle in others' territories.

*   People are part of the team when their contribution is needed; and when they're done, they're gone.

*   Within the team, there's a clear chain of command so that differences of opinion can be resolved within the team — i.e., self-managed teams.

Common approaches to coordinating business processes include business-process reengineering, and preaching the value of business partnership. The BWB paradigm suggests a far more effective approach: internal customer-supplier relations.

Business Process Reengineering

Business process reengineering (BPR) coordinates activities by pre-establishing the flow of work. The result is a procedure that maps an efficient series of steps taken to accomplish a given purpose. This flow chart then coordinates people's activities across organizational boundaries.

BPR invests significant effort in carefully planning the flow of work. Sufficient detail is needed before a procedure can serve as an effective coordinating mechanism.

Because the effort involved in planning a work flow is significant, BPR generally considers no more than a few major business processes. The result is an organization that's efficient at one or a few of its work flows, but less effective than ever at the remainder of its deliverables.

For example, the organization may trim the costs of its product or service manufacturing, but make it more difficult to do custom work or to introduce new products and services.

A more serious shortcoming is the rigid, assembly-line style of organization it produces. With BPR, the same team of people performs that process — even if it lacks the unique skills required by the particular project. Because the work flow is standardized, teams may not have access to specialists who are needed by one project but not by others.

Similarly, the sequence of tasks is fixed, along with the order in which they're done. Such rigid organizations don't do well at custom work, such as that done by most white-collar organizations where each project is somewhat different.

Furthermore, BPR defines what people *do,* not what they sell. It focuses people on tasks, not running lines of business that sell many different things to many different internal customers. This discourages innovation in how work gets done — counter to internal entrepreneurs who are always looking for a better way.

To compensate for this, BPR appoints a "process owner" — one person whose job is to improve the process over time. Of course, a single mind cannot accomplish as much as everybody continually improving their respective processes. Meanwhile, the process owner disempowers others as he or she tells them what to do.

Cleaning up work flows may sound simple, but a professional function is not a simple assembly line where teamwork can be preordained through a flow chart. Optimizing a few work flows for the sake of efficiency risks damaging the effectiveness of the entire organization.

Business Partners

Some have said that internal service providers should consider themselves "business partners" and share authority and account-ability with internal clients as equals. For example, IT should consider themselves part of the clients' business teams.

While it's believed that this will lead to good collaboration, in practice it generally leads to trouble. Accountabilities are unclear, and each party feels it has some authority over the other, leading to disempowerment and finger pointing.

Consider two perspectives:

*   Staff feel they have a right to tell clients how to run their businesses, and may feel accountable for forcing changes on clients. In the above example, IT staff may feel it's their job to make clients' technology decisions for them as if they were the customer for their own services.

*   Clients may feel they have the right to tell staff how to run their internal services business. Continuing the IT example,

clients may feel they have the right to tell the IT members of their team how to manage their technology projects.

Respecting one another's different domains and expertise is, in fact, a much better way to build healthy partnerships without any loss of commitment to one another's success.

The BWB paradigm builds effective partnerships through clear customer-supplier relations. Again, consider the two perspectives:

*   Staff respect customers' rights to make purchase decisions. For example, they present options with information about each (as in Chevrolet, Cadillac, and Rolls-Royce), then let customers decide which they'll buy.

*   Clients allow staff to run their internal businesses as they see fit. They decide what they'll buy, then leave it to the internal provider to figure out how to make the chosen product or service.

Clear but distinct accountabilities reduce disputes and finger pointing. Furthermore, synergies are gained when customers and suppliers recognize their different competencies, and each contributes what he or she knows without attempting to micromanage the other.

By the way, customer focus doesn't mean that staff passively take orders with little initiative in forwarding new ideas that might pay off for the company. There are many ways that entrepreneurs are proactive without usurping the customers' right to decide what they buy:

*   Internal entrepreneurs propose any new ideas they think will benefit their customers, and proactively share what they know.

*   Staff can be quite innovative in evolving their product lines, while still respecting customers' right to decide what they'll buy.

*   Staff proactively invest in their own businesses — in process improvements, technology innovation, and new products — to remain competitive.

The BWB Approach

The BWB paradigm suggests a powerful approach to cross-boundary work flows, one that applies within a department as well as across an entire corporation.

For each project or service, a clear organization chart should identify the one and only group that sells that deliverable. This group is considered the "prime contractor."

The first job of the prime contractor is to acquire needed help from subcontractors, i.e., from peers anywhere in the corporation.

Entrepreneurs have an incentive to draw others onto their project teams because they are more competitive when they utilize the services of specialists rather than attempt to do everything themselves.

Meanwhile, people have an incentive to help each other since internal customers (peer groups within the same department) are customers nonetheless, and it's important to please them.

Of course, subcontractors can, in turn, buy from other peers — their subcontractors. As each business within a business buys what it needs from its peers, teams form automatically, without the need for management intervention.

Since entrepreneurs only buy what they need for each particular project, teams draw on just the right people at just the right time. Business processes are clearly defined, and yet they're flexible and dynamic.

Even better, people buy products and services from one another, not just "warm bodies" to work on the project team. Thus, everyone takes responsibility for their individual deliverables, the sub-modules of the project.

Subcontracting for deliverables rather than people distributes the workload of managing the project. Subcontractors are project managers of their respective deliverables, and take responsibility for coordinating their own work as well as for arranging their suppliers.

This way, the prime contractor doesn't need to direct the detailed activities of everyone on the project team, an impossible challenge on large, complex projects. Instead, each layer coordinates only the next layer. Project management becomes much more feasible and reliable.

The BWB approach also enhances the quality of collaboration. People agree on what they can expect of one another; they respect others' skills and prerogatives; they refrain from micromanaging peers or stepping on others' territories; and they willingly support peers who are their customers.

Internal buy-sell transactions need not be bureaucratic with extensive paperwork. A simple memo of understanding can clarify who is buying what from whom, and is always good business practice.

Also, the BWB approach does not assume or require an actual transfer of funds (i.e., chargebacks). With or without chargebacks, there's nothing to prevent each group from thinking in the terms of being a business within a business.

In summary, treating peers as customers and suppliers builds flexible but explicit cross-boundary work flows, clear individual accountability, healthy collaboration, and close partnerships based on mutual interdependence.

7. Implications for Governance

The word "governance" refers to the ways an organization coordinates and controls the resources and actions of the various groups within it.

Unfortunately, for lack of understanding of the systemic forces at work in organizations, many people assume that control can only be accomplished by positioning one group to oversee another.

This approach is dangerous. It invariably separates authority from accountability, giving one group power over another group's line of business. Internal tensions are inevitable. But more serious problems also occur.

Those having authority without concomitant accountability often become tyrants, ruling whimsically with little regard for the challenges of running the business. Who's to control the controllers?

In other cases, those with authority get blamed for the misbehavior of the people they're supposed to control — the "whipping boy" for others' mistakes. Why should others act responsibly when there's another group that's supposed to be in control and will take the blame?

On the other hand, those holding accountability but without matching authority become disempowered victims and scapegoats, unable to run their businesses as they see fit, demoralized and disenfranchised, and both unwilling and unable to lend their creative energy to improving the organization.

Three common examples of such problems are: when internal service providers are asked to control their customers; when executive committees are set up to oversee a function; and when an Audit function oversees its peers.

Staff Oversight

Often, corporate executives expect internal service organizations to perform a control function, giving staff the power to approve clients' purchase decisions or control clients' spending. For example, it's not uncommon to ask Corporate Finance to approve others' spending, and Corporate IT staff to judge and approve all requests for personal computers or for software packages.

Using staff to control their customers is absolutely counter to the BWB paradigm.

Whenever internal entrepreneurs judge or control their customers, two things happen:

1. Clients learn to see them as an obstacle, not an ally.

2. Staff lose sight of customer focus. They come to believe that they know what's best for the company, and learn to see clients as unruly renegades instead of as customers who pay their bills — the opposite of an entrepreneurial, customer-focused service function.

This control-oriented relationship undermines the partnership that's built through respectful customer-supplier relations. Without a close working relationship, staff are unlikely to make significant contributions to clients' business strategies. In other words, using staff to control their clients undermines their primary mission of delivering products and services that add value to the business.

The BWB paradigm suggests an alternative. Corporate controls are exercised through *line* management, not through staff functions. Commands flow through the hierarchy where they carry legitimate authority, not laterally via staff.

For example, if you want to control IT spending, don't ask the IT department to filter clients' requests. Instead, give clients limited spending power and hold them to their budgets.

If you want to ensure that IT procurements follow standards, hold clients responsible for their purchase decisions and for gaining approval from their chain of command for any necessary variances.

Using the legitimate authority of the hierarchy to exercise control is far more effective. People listen to their bosses, though they may look for ways around peers who are impediments.

And, in the long run, it will give staff more, not less, influence. When internal entrepreneurs remain customer focused and earn market share by becoming the vendor of choice, they're better able to guide clients toward corporate standards and policies than they could picking fights with clients who have their own agendas.

Executive Steering Committees

Another common mechanism of governance is the executive steering committee: a team of executives formed to oversee a function.

Often, the purpose and boundaries of these committees are unclear. As a result, executive steering committees may disempower the organization's leadership, blunt the staff's entrepreneurial spirit, and create a bureaucratic obstacle to innovation.

It's not that executive committees are inherently bad. It's that committee *oversight* is bad.

Again, the right approach is control via the legitimate authority of the hierarchy.

A business within a business reports to a boss whose job is to evaluate and manage the department. Evaluations should be based on input from clients, subordinates, and internal suppliers — as in 360-degree reviews. Evaluations can include both quantitative metrics (like market share and cost comparisons) and subjective assessments (like customer satisfaction).

Once performance-management processes are clearly established, the role of committees becomes clearer. The following types of committees might be useful to a business within a business:

* **Board:** An internal "board of directors" to help the business within a business succeed. Like any good corporate Board, they do not micromanage the executive, but instead add value by reviewing major strategic decisions and coaching the executive on key business and leadership issues.

* **Purser:** A committee that owns a "checkbook" of spending power, such as the portion of the department's budget designated for client-benefitting products and services. A purser committee represents the client community as a whole, and makes purchase decisions by setting priorities from among the requests of the many clients they represent.

   The keeps staff out of the conflict of interests that arises when they set their own priorities, i.e., make clients' purchase decisions for them.

   A purser committee manages a specific checkbook. It does not have the power to control other sales, e.g., when a business unit uses its own budget to buy additional things from the department.

* **Consortium:** An identified set of clients who together purchase a specific product or service. Members must speak with one voice as if they were a single customer, sharing decision making, costs, and ownership of the results.

   A consortium is distinct from the market as a whole, which includes any and all clients and does not identify which clients will purchase a given product.

* **User group:** An association of people who use a given product or service. They meet to exchange information that will assist in their getting value from the product.

   A user group is distinct from a consortium in that each member of the user group can/did purchase the product independently; they do not share a single contract with the organization.

*   **Focus group:** A team of people representing potential customers who share their values, opinions, and ideas to guide the research and product-development activities of the organization. They meet at the request of the organization, and answer questions provided by the organization. They do not make decisions for the organization.

*   **Professional community:** If a function is decentralized, the set of executives who manage the various groups, or the set of managers of a specific sub-discipline. They meet to share their experiences, share research and product development, agree on standards and policies, and further the interests of the profession.

Many of the above types of committees may be helpful, and the same individuals may belong to multiple committees. However, it's essential that their purposes be kept distinct.

For example, a conflict of interests is created when a single committee attempts to be both a Board (helping the department succeed) and a Purser (demanding customers who want more for less).

Audit

While an internal market combined with the traditional functions of the management hierarchy provide most of the necessary controls, there are cases where an Audit function is warranted.

Audit is not the same as quality inspection. In the spirit of total quality management, quality inspection is the responsibility of every producing function. It should be done every day in the normal course of doing business, not occasionally by outsiders. Therefore, quality inspection is not an appropriate role for Auditors.

Rather, Audit performs *checks to ensure that people are complying with rules and policies.*

Since Audit is inherently disempowering, it should be used sparingly, only when other mechanisms of governance cannot work. Specifically, Audit is needed when compliance depends strictly on honesty — that is, where intrinsic checks and balances are inadequate or altogether missing. The following are examples of appropriate uses of an Audit function:

* **Unchecked power:** when people can use their position and power for personal gain.

For example, an organization may audit the financial statements of its managers if people are in a position to embezzle money or extort personal concessions from vendors.

As always, the most effective controls are systemic: checks and balances built into financial processes. If this isn't possible, then Audit is legitimately required.

* **Missing metrics:** when customers cannot perceive the quality of the products they buy until well after the purchase.

For example, clients may not be able to know whether a technical product complies with standards.

A legitimate role of Audit is to provide customers with the information they need to be smart buyers, but not to demand that customers always buy the highest quality (Rolls-Royce) solutions.

* **Conflicting stakeholders:** when customers' interests deviate from the interests of other stakeholders.

For example, IT may be caught in a bind. Customers in specific business units want customized solutions, while shareholders want standardization and shared solutions to save money.

The root cause of this predicament is a customer whose interests are not aligned with those of the shareholders. The right answer is to better align customers' metrics and rewards.

For example, if business units paid the full cost of customization, and if the savings from sharing with peers accrued to their bottom lines, then they'd only buy unique solutions when the benefits of customization warranted the incremental costs.

If alignment cannot be accomplished systemically, Audit may be used to examine *customers'* purchase decisions, but never to control internal service providers.

Unfortunately, Audit tends to be used too freely. Whenever control is an issue, some executives would rather appoint an Auditor than think through more appropriate systemic governance mechanisms. Consider the following cases where Audit is misused:

* **Altruism:**   when people are expected to act against their own best interests.

For example, managers may be expected to reduce costs, while their job grade and salary depend on the size of their empires.

Audit is then used to force people to address objectives that are against their own best interests.

Audit is rarely appropriate here. A far better answer is to align incentive systems such that serving one's customers is in one's own best interests.

* **Unreasonable laws:**   when people are required to act against anyone's best interests.

For example, regulations do not allow government employees to serve refreshments at their all-day meetings for fear that they will spend taxpayers' money on lavish meals. Instead, their meetings involve longer breaks so that people can go to a cafeteria, resulting in costly losses of productivity.

A responsible manager may want to violate the rule and do what is, in fact, in the best interests of taxpayers. Therefore, Auditors are required to ensure that people follow unreasonable rules rather than do what they deem right.

Unreasonable laws within corporations occur when bureaucrats attempt to micro-manage employees behaviors rather than regulate outcomes. A better approach is to manage people by results, and build the necessary feedback loops to measure those results.

* **Externalities:** where some of the costs of a purchase are not borne by the customers who make (and benefit from) the purchase decision.

In the environment, pollution is the result of the lack of any costs associated with using up clean air or water. Within corporations, an example is legal risk; a business unit may take unacceptable risks if the costs of litigation are born by the corporate legal department, not the business unit.

The traditional response is regulation, enforced through Audit. This leads to a cat-and-mouse game where people are given incentives to push the limits of the regulations and get away with whatever they can.

A better approach is to internalize those externalities. In the environmental example, this is done by charging corporations a fee for pollution. In the example of legal risk, business units should absorb the costs of any litigation resulting from their misbehavior.

Of course, the most economic answer is not zero pollution, or zero legal risk. The costs of perfect compliance may far outweigh the risks of non-compliance. When a systemic feedback loop is built, the market will automatically lead everyone to find the right balance.

When there are situations that legitimately require Auditors, the Audit function must be carefully chartered to avoid problems.

Audit should never be used to substitute for direction through line management. The order to comply with rules and policies must come through one's chain of command, as should the directive to cooperate with Auditors. Without such legitimacy, Auditors will have a difficult time doing their jobs and compliance will be minimal. Auditors check on compliance; they do not replace managers by setting objectives or giving orders.

Auditors report on compliance, but they do not diagnose the root causes of problems or recommend corrective actions. No matter how bright individual Auditors may be, they cannot hope to know a function as well as the many people who do the job day after day. Their suggestions may not be as good as solutions the group itself designs to address the issue.

Furthermore, if Auditors suggest solutions, they risk conflicts of interests. Their influential position makes it hard to do anything but follow their suggestions. Imagine an IRS agent suggesting a particular brand of accounting software!

Auditors may judge decisions made (or proposed) by others, for example, whether an investment in a line of business is wise. However, they must never *make* any business decisions for those they audit, such as how much a group should invest in a line of business. Doing so disempowers internal entrepreneurs, and unfairly imposes risks on them.

For example, in one state government, "performance audits" dictated how many people a group could hire for specific functions. These caps forced the group to reduce its quality of service and turn away valuable business. Of course, these consequence were blamed on the group, not on the Auditors.

In general, Auditors must not hold any authority over others or control others' activities. Doing so would disempower others and make it impossible to hold managers accountable for their own results. It's easy to image someone saying, "The Auditor made me do this; our poor performance is their fault."

A well aligned organization built on the BWB paradigm systemically provides most of the needed controls. Audit is needed when information can only be produced by human inspections.

Appropriate Governance

Since governance means the *mechanisms* of coordination and control, there's no need to assume that people have to do it. With the exception of the management hierarchy, using people to coordinate and control others should be considered a governance mechanism of last resort.

The BWB paradigm suggests alternative forms of governance: the mechanisms of a market economy. When governance is systemic, it's comprehensive, detailed, ever-present, context-specific, flexible, and effective.

8. Autonomous Business Units Versus Corporate Synergies

Corporations are often comprised of a number of autonomous business units. To be held accountable for their bottom lines, business unit leaders must be given control of all their costs.

Some people believe this warrants decentralization of service functions such as engineering, manufacturing, procurement, sales, communications, information systems, finance, human resources, real estate, and administration — any business within a business which is not directly accountable for product lines.

These folks will be quick to add that centralized "shared services" organizations often view themselves as monopolies with no need to be customer focused.

Staff who think this way generate costly bureaucracies, and are insensitive to the unique needs of their diverse clients.

Worse, they may believe they carry the power of the corporation, and have the right to make decisions for clients and control clients' decision making.

If they behave this way, then shared-services organizations become the antithesis of autonomous business units. The answer, these people argue, is to give each business unit the functions it needs to support its business.

While on the surface this may sound logical, the truth is that decentralization is extremely expensive.

Decentralization has three major consequences: 3

*   **Lost economies of scale:** Many small departments cannot gain the economies of scale of a consolidated function with its shared infrastructure and shared licenses.

    There are also economies in pooling requirements for partial headcount (where two business units each need a half-time specialist), and in smoothing workload (where one business unit's peak demand is another's valley), also lost through decentralization.

    A fragmented function loses negotiating position, both purchasing power (e.g., volume discounts) and selling power (the strength in selling a broad product line).

    Economies are also lost when isolated professionals are less likely to share their experiences and expertise. There is less opportunity for reusing knowledge, research, and solutions, leading to costly reinvention.

*   **Reduced specialization:** Small decentralized groups cannot specialize to the same degree as can a consolidated function. Decentralized staff must be relative generalists to do everything their business units need.

    By contrast, a centralized function can establish groups of specialists that are shared throughout the corporation.

    The results of lost specialization (i.e., less professional depth in each discipline) are a slower pace of innovation, reduced productivity and responsiveness, lower quality, and limited career paths that may not attract top talent.

---

3.   For a detailed analysis of the trade-offs of decentralization, see: Meyer, N. Dean. *Decentralization: Fantasies, Failings, and Fundamentals.*

*   **Lost corporatewide synergies:** Business units that could be synergistic collaborate less as a result of decentralization.

Conversely, shared support functions improve business units' synergies.

For example, a shared engineering function can reduce the variety of parts in use (e.g., nuts and bolts) to a standard set, driving down every business unit's procurement, inventory, manufacturing, and repair costs.

Shared HR services can lead to more flexible staffing.

Shared information systems can facilitate cross-boundary work flows, and business synergies such as a common view of external customers.

A common financial chart of accounts can induce better corporatewide resource management.

All such opportunities for business synergies are diminished through decentralization.

A corporation may accept these as the "inevitable" costs of business-unit autonomy, but there's no need. The BWB paradigm breaks the apparent paradox. It allows business units to remain autonomous while sharing service functions.

Consider an analogy. You demand absolute control over what you eat. That's entirely reasonable. Yet you probably don't own your own grocery store. Instead, you share a centralized grocery store with your community.

You don't feel the need to own a grocery store since you control your spending power. You buy what you want, and don't buy things that don't seem worthwhile to you.

Of course, if you don't find what you want at your usual grocery store and the store is unwilling to order it for you, you have the right to go to another store. But, for most of us, doing so is the exception rather than the rule; we frequent our usual store, and shop elsewhere only on occasion for unusual items.

You're able to control what you eat without owning your own store because we live in a *market economy,* and grocery stores are customer focused and work hard to supply you with just what you want (and will pay for).

Similarly, autonomous business units are in complete control of what they buy from external vendors. In a BWB organization, they're equally in control of internal vendors.

Entrepreneurial support functions treat business units as customers; only sell what business units choose to buy; customize their products and services to the extent that business units are willing to pay; and treat business units as well as they would if they reported to the business-unit executive.

In addition, they give business units a better deal than could be gotten from a fragmented set of small groups of generalists.

In short, the BWB paradigm allows a corporation to "have its cake and eat it too." Product managers and support services alike can be managed as autonomous business units, in complete control of their costs and their strategies. At the same time, centralized shared-services providers can deliver cost savings and synergies.

9. Benefits

The BWB paradigm brings out the best in staff, and induces the best business decisions for the organization and for the corporation as a whole. Consider its benefits:

* **Recognizing internal customers** creates a culture of customer focus, and enhances partnerships and communications.

* **Clearly defining products and "contracts"** brings about a results orientation, and clearly specifies accountabilities for results, prices, and delivery times.

* **Respect for customers' purchase decisions** automatically ensures strategic alignment throughout the corporation.

   Instead of vague plans, committees, and decrees which ask providers to guess what their customers might need, internal customers will use their limited spending power to buy just what they most need to accomplish their strategies. This maximizes ROI.

* **Using the internal value chain rather than top-down plans** adjusts the internal economy — what each organization does for whom — dynamically throughout the year, allowing the corporation to realign resources quickly and flexibly as strategies shift in turbulent times.

* **Treating peers as internal suppliers** provides a mechanism for flexible, dynamic cross-boundary teamwork. Everyone buys from peers just what they need to get their jobs done. This is much more flexible and effective than pre-defined business processes.

* **Recognizing peers as customers** improves the quality and customer focus of internal support staff. It also encourages all groups to sell their products and services to others within the

organization just as they do to clients outside the organization, eliminating the "cobbler's children" syndrome where the organization is the last to utilize its own products and services.

* **Viewing internal support functions as businesses** eliminates two classes of citizenship (operational versus support functions), and brings efficiency and innovation to what some might call "back room" functions.

* **The pressure of competition (internal and external)** makes everyone frugal, to ensure that they're delivering the best value and growing their market share. Top-down cost-cutting edicts are replaced with cost-conscious decision making at every level, on every issue, every day, maximizing the organization's returns on investments.

* **Earning market share through performance** makes each group an internal vendor of choice. This reduces pressure for expensive decentralization and outsourcing.

* **Managing staff by their P&L rather than expense caps** allows internal entrepreneurs to respond to new, high-payoff opportunities rather than being resource-constrained obstacles to customers' business objectives; and it encourages staff to be innovative about offering new, high-payoff products and services.

* **Viewing contractors and vendors as extensions to internal staff** makes the best use of insiders and outsiders in every case, all the time (unlike massive, monolithic outsourcing studies).

Whenever vendors and contractors offer a better value, internal entrepreneurs are the first to offer outsiders as part of their product line. And when vendors are brought in through the appropriate internal staff, those in the profession manage their external colleagues, ensuring compliance with corporate standards and policies.

*   **The feeling of ownership of a business** motivates people to do all they can to improve the organization, including performing at their own peaks.

*   **The entreprenuerial spirit** gets everyone thinking about improving current processes; innovating to keep current products and services up to date; and inventing new products and services that might contribute to customers' businesses.

*   **Fulfilling, whole jobs** engage the creative thinking of everyone in the organization.

    People are motivated by more than just money; they work to seek self-fulfillment, to contribute meaningfully to worthwhile purposes, and to enjoy social interactions. BWB organizations offer all these motivators. By becoming employers of choice, BWB organizations attract and retain the best talent in a way that obviates hiring bidding wars.

*   **The experience of running a small business** cultivates the next generation of corporate leaders.

The positive effects of the BWB paradigm are lasting, not fleeting, because they're based on systemic change. Unlike strategic plans, leadership development programs, and executive exhortations and commands, implementing a BWB organization maximizes everybody's performance, on every front, forevermore.

10. Implementation

Implementing the BWB paradigm requires more than communicating the vision. It requires systemic changes in the organization, and meticulous management of change.

Even when people want to do the right things, an organization may put obstacles in their way. Here's a common example:

> *As an internal entrepreneur, you want to offer your customers the best value, so you know you should make every effort to keep your costs down.*
>
> *But imagine that you work in an organization where your political stature, your title, and your paycheck all depend on how big an "empire" you run — more headcount leads to a higher job grade. Essentially, the company is paying you to maximize, not minimize, your costs!*

Organizations produce myriad signals that guide everyone's day-to-day decisions and actions. Some are appropriate, many are unclear and confusing, some may be conflicting, and a few may be perverse (as is rewarding people for empire building).

These signals determine the style of the organization, and make or break its performance.

If these signals guide people back to bureaucratic processes and behaviors, communicating the vision will inevitably lead to frustration and cynicism.

Only when an organization's signals are supportive can staff truly perform as empowered internal entrepreneurs.

Beyond just removing disincentives to entrepreneurship, a carefully designed set of organizational signals is fundamental to the implementation of the BWB paradigm.

When the signals are well aligned, they automatically control and coordinate people; so other mechanisms of control are less needed. In other words, a well designed organization permits empowerment without any loss of control.

A BWB organization depends on replacing top-down control, auditors, and bureaucracy with a well designed set of organizational signals that enable the empowerment of internal entrepreneurs.

BWB and Organizational Design

The BWB paradigm provides a philosophy that guides the design of a consistent, comprehensive, healthy set of signals.

For example, if a leader is concerned about clients' expectations outstripping available resources, she might focus on the project-approval process.

In traditional organizations, she might implement a series of staff reviews to filter out unworthy projects, and a client steering committee to set priorities.

The problem is that staff then become adversarial hurdles who audit and judge clients' ideas — the opposite of customer focus. And the organization as a whole is viewed as bureaucratic and difficult to do business with.

In the BWB paradigm, she'd solve the problem quite differently. She wouldn't discourage her staff's entrepreneurial enthusiasm for selling clients as much as possible, constrained only by clients' ability to pay. And she certainly wouldn't want to risk her market share by sacrificing the organization's customer focus.

Instead, this leader might establish resource-tracking processes that show clients how much is left in their "checkbook." Then, it becomes the clients' job to live within their means and to decide which projects are funded. Staff never have to judge or reject their clients. And clients, who know their business needs best, set priorities.

In this example, the BWB paradigm guided us to a market solution rather than bureaucracy.

While the BWB paradigm guides organizational design, the relationship is symbiotic in that, by redesigning an organization, leaders can implement the BWB paradigm. Consider another example:

BWB guides organizational design: Say you want to improve teamwork. the BWB paradigm suggests a project-management process that defines a prime contractor for each project, who then "hires" subcontractors from among peer groups — buying products and services from subcontractors, not just staff's time to do as they're told.

Organizational design implements BWB: The project-management process gets people to define their jobs as selling products and services to peers within the department, to clients throughout the company, and to external customers. This change moves staff closer to the BWB paradigm.

"You can't legislate the human heart."

Anonymous

The way to implement the BWB paradigm is not by exhortation, but rather by the thoughtful design of the organizational environment.

Five Organizational Systems

How can leaders who wish to implement the BWB paradigm redesign an organization?

There are five organizational systems that produce most of the signals that guide people's work, portrayed in Figure 1.

By adjusting these five organizational systems, leaders can convert hierarchical, bureaucratic organizations into a dynamic marketplace of vibrant businesses within a business.

Figure 1: Five Organizational Systems *4*

* **Culture:** the habits and values practiced throughout the organization.

* **Structure:** the organization chart that determines staff's lines of business, and the work flows that combine various specialists into project teams.

* **Internal economy:** the resource management processes, including budgeting, rate setting, purchase decisions, and tracking processes.

* **Methods and tools:** the capabilities of the various entrepreneurships.

* **Metrics and rewards:** the feedback staff get, and the consequences of their performance.

---

4.   The five organizational systems and the RoadMap transformational process are described in detail in: Meyer, N. Dean. *RoadMap: how to understand, diagnose, and fix your organization.*

Transformation Strategy

Successful implementation of the BWB paradigm requires carefully designed changes in the five organizational systems, sequenced in the proper order, and implemented at a reasonable pace.

Implementation begins with planning the transformation strategy: what changes are needed, and what is the proper sequence?

The transformation planning process itself is of value. Leaders explore the implications of the BWB paradigm for their organization, and translate the concept into a clear, detailed vision of their goal — a high-performance organization.

"We don't have the time to do it quickly!"

Dave Anderson
President, American Family Insurance

Based on this clearly defined vision of how the organization should work, they assess the gaps in the current organization, building their commitment to change.

Gaps are traced to root causes — the five organizational systems — and the proper sequence of changes is determined.

Then, with each step in the transformation process, the organization moves closer to its vision, and it experiences more and more of the powerful benefits of customer focus, entrepreneurship, and empowerment.

11. Leadership

This story ends where it begins.... Real leadership is not coming up with great business strategies, or making all the tough business decisions. *Everybody* in the organization should think about strategy, and everybody should make decisions about their own businesses within a business.

In a well designed organization, empowered entrepreneurs who make independent decisions are automatically coordinated and aligned with corporate strategies by the very nature of the environment, by the consistent signals they get.

Not only does this eliminate the need for expensive, restrictive bureaucracy and controls. It unleashes everybody's creativity, and fills the organization with energy and commitment.

Meanwhile, executives can focus on leadership, not doing their managers' jobs for them.

In short, true leaders rally staff around a compelling vision of the ideal organization — the BWB paradigm.

Then, they implement that vision by deliberately adjusting the signals that guide people, using science to design each of the five organizational systems.

In doing so, leaders develop organizations in which everyone can succeed, with or without them — organizations in which every small group is managed as its own independent, yet interdependent, business within a business.